Daughter of the Earth

Kavisha Prajapati

BookLeaf Publishing

India | USA | UK

Presentation by *BookLeaf Publishing*

Web: www.bookleafpub.com

E-mail: info@bookleafpub.com

ISBN: 9789360948375

First edition 2024

Origins

There was a time I walked this Earth alone.
Wandering from forest to forest,
exploring evergreen

The trees were my companion
Constant and sturdy, but immovable
Spirits uplifted every time I sat graced by their
shade.

I was born from the mud,
Crafted with leaves, fruit, pollen,
Pachamama's abundance.

Sculpted by the wind
Whose force runs with direction and intention.

I was given life by the flame of the fire
And woke up in the dark of the night,

Eyes ablaze,
Body poised,
Ready to move mountains

Mind ignited
With consciousness, reality, and perception.

Dreaming, Naturally

I wish I were a sparrow
Jostling through the leaves
Fritting from one branch to another
Chirping like I invented music

I wish I were a tree
Housing an array of birds, bugs, and bumblebees
All buzzing with efficiency and sustenance

I wish I were a steward living in a community
who tends to the Earth,
For she is the nature of plenty and we are her
children
Destined to celebrate her creations

Above It All

The sky at transition is always
The most beautiful thing.

The magic of the sun
Erupts in a never-ending rhythm of color –
Dancing to the divine rhythms of the universe.

Grounding the self on Earth is a chore
When your line of sight is perceiving a bird
Fly its way into the horizon,

Elevated in the stratosphere
Is where we find the joyous of chirps,
The intimate sound heard only by
The tips of the trees and the great unknown.

Fall is a Feeling

the last bits of summer sun simmer down
into an orange fire nestled in the living room

greens turn into yellow turn into reds
and the freshness of trees leaves its taste in a
bushel of apples

the air is never stale and heavy
but fresh and crisp with the fleeting essence of a
change in pace

I can bake bread just to have its fragrance linger
one day, I wore a thin layer of sleeves
the next, a bundle of scarves

and when I opened my eyes
the warmth had come and gone
scattered throughout the atmosphere
leaving in its wake, an icy haze

Hold My Hand

The goodness comes naturally
Like birds in the morning
Stay there for a while...
I know the chaos is real
Not a figment of the imagination
Go outside and play, whenever you want
Don't lose yourself
In the dreams behind closed eyes
I'll tell you -
What's real is the tiny human who calls you
didi*
And the quiet moments between giggles
They carry the warmth of home
Stay there for a while...
Breathe it in deeply, fully,
You are connected
Let the unseen support you
Shower you with blessings and new beginnings
Gifts generosity and grace
Be like a sloth
Patient, slow, smiling :)
But don't forget
To thank yourself

*big sister

Daughter of the Earth

If you ever
lay your hands on me
with the intention of
conquering my body
like it's a territory to seize
in the insatiable battle
of infinite desire
just know
you will never win
because your temptation
stems from an unhonorable place.

the will to control
the will to hold power over another sentient
being
is quite weak actually.
it is a lack of control over the self
and amnesia
over the sanctity of humanity.

let me warn you
that im protected
by forces larger than human life
just know
you will never win

because

the roots under the surface of my earth
will smother your air
branches will fence
with your brittle bones
and the ground underneath will open up,
devouring you whole.

Recollection

my body holds stories
it holds memories
if my body was unraveled like a piece of
developing film
it would showcase a series of moments over
time
moments that speak to warmth, belonging,
togetherness, visceral evolution, quiet
transformation, silent observation, wide-eyed
wonder, boisterous fun, hearty laughter,
willingness, determined action, and

Rules

Don't talk to me rude because I'll wither
like the petals off a flower in the heat spell

Don't yell when I give you my heart
because I'll be set ablaze and crumble into ash

Don't manipulate the script to make it seem like
I am the villain
Because truth boomerangs back with a feisty
vengeance

Don't say I didn't warn you

Blasphemy of Shakespeare

What is in a name? A rose would smell sweet
being called a poppy.
It would smell just as sweet being called a
puppy.

A puppy would bound just as happily
Towards the hands carrying its food
When it is called puppy
And when it is called cat.

A cat does not know
The name of its human companion
Whether their name is Jack or Rose,
Because it cannot understand.

I was named Shrishti.
My classmates called me Drishti.
To them, it did not matter
That a single letter
Could define the nature
Between our cultural nomenclatures.

What is in a name?
That which is foreign will still be foreign when
it is mispronounced.

The tongue will seduce only the language it is
familiar with
But the weary ear will still hear the message that
is meant for it.

I love Drishti,
Drishti signifies concentrated intention –
Powerful and intelligence embodied
But when I am Drishti,
I am sunk by the iceberg of invisibility.

I am Shrishti.
I am as expansive as infinity,
As never-ending as pi,
As undefined as the galaxy.

I matter because I am matter
Combined with energy, I am the Universe.
I am Shrishti.

So do not recite to me,
What is in a name?
Before getting to know mine.

Earth Justice

Our roots are deep
So deep we don't even understand how far they
go
Into the earth they flow
But in return, we don't let her grow?
We
abuse
misuse
her heart
her creations
We soil and destroy
Eat art
Consume poison
Romanticize space
Forgetting the biggest beauty is her
Is here

Our ancestors said
Do not bite the hand that feeds you
Give it tender love and care
Everything from the earth is a wish fulfilment

Heal Mama Earth, Heal
Let's tend to you better

Notes on Friendship

I march along in mid-air
Triumphantly to the tune of my own song

And there across the horizon,
I see a friend!

Different song but similar dance
So we meet at a stop

Where we rest and eat,
Joke and jive,
Smile and share
Just as long as the moment allows

We have dug our roots in that moment
But that moment is not infinite,
It too shall pass

And we will continue on our merry way
Full of fulfilment

Companionship is sacred
and that moment, A Gift

For whenever we meet

We will reconnect

We twirl onwards
But they are always there
Cheering me on

Are You With Me?

i am an artist

i see the world

through a lens of stories and color

wonder and imagination

borderline delusion?

head in the clouds

feet on the ground

running towards the vision

feeling free while i do so

i don't want to run alone

this light can bring others in too

Have You Met Yourself Yet?

Diamond studded velvet sky going towards
infinity

Stillness in the darkness illuminating the way to
freedom

The earth holds me with her tender arms.

Palms faced upwards, eyes looking inwards

The wind whistles tunes of my ancestors
transcending their graves.

I don't know where my mind ends and the
atmosphere begins

Constellations of memories of self-inflicted
wounds,

So I sing life into them – peace, breath, and life

Release them like birds uncaged.

The ocean carries my heart towards an
unidentified location

Traveling but not lost

The World and Me

That moment when the breeze

Comes to tickle my cheek

Reminds me that nature is alive.

Life is nothing short of beautiful

No one can persuade me

That the change of seasons isn't magic.

Or that the species and ecosystems underwater

Are not representative of creations

In a galaxy orchestrated by development.

Particles inside each of us destroy and recombine

An infinite number of times-

An elemental dance.

Am I not a reflection of the same mechanisms?

I can change my genetic makeup

By treating my body with better food

And have the freedom to partake

In wonderous adventures

All in pursuit of personal evolution.

Different versions of me

Die and others are reborn

Like a cycle of waves on the shore.

Like seasons of the self,

We truly are the universe experiencing itself.

Sacred Geometry

Focusing on the divine rhythms of the universe
and how they combust inside
Underneath my eyes
the way things are spirals
Rather than lines
but by drawing small lines
We can rise

The feeling of being protected
bombarding with the feeling
Of not needing to be protected from anything
the expansion of being uplifted
Where space is taken up with planets
and stars larger than Mars
Balanced out with the rooting of my feet
deep into the earth

Standing atop the pillars of duality
opening my eyes
To a reality just beginning

When I Saw the Sea

I sang to the ocean
It ebbed with the emotions in my voice

I listened to the ocean
The sheer power of the waves crashing on the
shore
In tune with the winds

I could bear it no more,
I ran to the ocean
And dove right in

I wanted to stay forever in the ocean
Tumbling in and out of the current
Surfacing only to see orange hues
Bobbing in between worlds
Cradling me through the passing of time

An Ode to the Half Moon

An ode to the moon
when a little less than full
is an ode of sweet acceptance
to the dark existence woven inside everything
that is whole

-- keep shining --

Divine Timing

life is a symphony and i am the conductor
the breath of the cosmos is the bass and i am the
melody
progressing in tandem with my internal world
flowing because the present takes direction from
the past to create the future
there are no mistakes,
just evolution